CAROLINA
PANTHERS

by Brian Joura

Published by ABDO Publishing Company, 8000 West 78th Street, Edina, Minnesota 55439. Copyright © 2011 by Abdo Consulting Group, Inc. International copyrights reserved in all countries. No part of this book may be reproduced in any form without written permission from the publisher. SportsZone™ is a trademark and logo of ABDO Publishing Company.

Printed in the United States of America, North Mankato, Minnesota
062010
092010

Editor: Matt Tustison
Copy Editor: Nicholas Cafarelli
Interior Design and Production: Kazuko Collins
Cover Design: Kazuko Collins

Photo Credits: Brian Blanco/AP Images, cover; Paul Spinelli/AP Images, title page; Dave Martin/AP Images, 4; Mark J. Terrill/AP Images, 7, 8; Amy Sancetta/AP Images, 11; Chuck Burton/AP Images, 12, 19, 20, 34, 42 (bottom), 43 (bottom); Karen Tam/AP Images, 15, 42 (top); Alan Marler/AP Images, 16, 42 (middle); Rusty Burroughs/AP Images, 24; Nell Redmond/AP Images, 22, 41, 47; Bill Kostroun/AP Images, 26, 43 (middle); Rick Havner/AP Images, 29, 37, 39, 43 (top); Charles Rex Arbogast/AP Images, 31; Kathy Willens/AP Photos, 32; John Todd/AP Images, 44

Library of Congress Cataloging-in-Publication Data
Joura, Brian.
  Carolina Panthers / Brian Joura.
     p. cm. — (Inside the NFL)
  Includes index.
  ISBN 978-1-61714-005-1
  1. Carolina Panthers (Football team)—History—Juvenile literature. I. Title.
  GV956.C27J68 2011
  796.332'640975676—dc22
                                    2010013676

TABLE OF CONTENTS

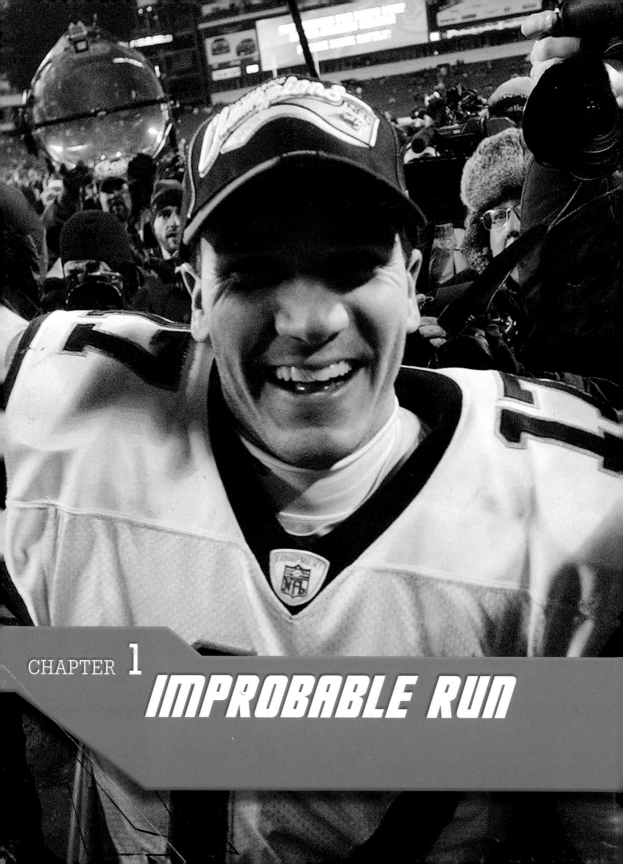

CHAPTER 1

IMPROBABLE RUN

T

he Carolina Panthers finished 1–15 in 2001. It was the worst record in the National Football League (NFL). Only two seasons later, though, the Panthers had improved a lot. They could compete with any team in the league. They were led by a quarterback whose success surprised many football followers.

The Panthers' trip to the Super Bowl after the 2003 season remains the brightest highlight in team history. Quarterback Jake Delhomme was one of the stars. He had played at the tiny University of Southwestern Louisiana. He entered the 1997 NFL Draft but was not taken by any team. It was a long road to NFL success for Delhomme. He did not become a starter until in 2003 with the Panthers.

Delhomme led Carolina against quarterback Tom Brady and the mighty New England Patriots in Super Bowl XXXVIII. The Patriots were seven-point

QUARTERBACK JAKE DELHOMME CELEBRATES AFTER CAROLINA DEFEATED PHILADELPHIA 14–3 IN THE NFC CHAMPIONSHIP GAME IN JANUARY 2004.

JAKE DELHOMME

Quarterback Jake Delhomme began his NFL career as an undrafted free agent with the New Orleans Saints in 1997. He spent a season on the Saints' practice squad. New Orleans then assigned him to the NFL Europe league to gain experience. He helped the Frankfurt Galaxy win World Bowl VII in June 1999.

The Saints brought Delhomme back as a backup quarterback. He saw little playing time through 2002.

The Panthers thought he had potential, however, and signed Delhomme. With Carolina trailing the Jacksonville Jaguars 17–0 in the 2003 opener, coach John Fox put Delhomme in the game. In relief of Rodney Peete, Delhomme threw three touchdown passes and led Carolina to a 24–23 win.

Delhomme started the rest of the season. The Panthers went 11–5, won the National Football Conference (NFC) South Division, and made a magical playoff run.

favorites on February 1, 2004, at Reliant Stadium in Houston, Texas. The Panthers were not just satisfied with being in the "big game," though. They thought they could win it.

The Patriots had won the Super Bowl two years earlier and were expected by most people to win this time too. They went 14–2 in the regular season. The Panthers had gone 11–5 in the regular season. But Carolina stood toe to toe with New England.

After a scoreless first quarter, the teams traded touchdowns at the end of the second quarter. Delhomme and wide receiver Steve Smith connected on a 39-yard

CAROLINA'S DESHAUN FOSTER DIVES PAST NEW ENGLAND SAFETY RODNEY HARRISON TO COMPLETE A 33-YARD TOUCHDOWN RUN IN SUPER BOWL XXXVIII.

CAROLINA PANTHERS

touchdown pass. The play capped a 95-yard drive. The Panthers tied the game at 7–7. Then, as time expired in the first half, Carolina's John Kasay kicked a 50-yard field goal. This cut New England's lead to 14–10.

Neither team scored in the third quarter. But then came one of the most thrilling finishes in Super Bowl history.

The Patriots scored first, putting them up 21–10. But the Panthers clawed back with three big plays to take the lead.

DeShaun Foster scored on a 33-yard run for the first big play. Carolina's two-point conversion try failed. It looked as if the Patriots were going to score again. However, cornerback Reggie Howard came up with the second big play by inter-cepting a pass from Brady in the end zone. Stuck deep in its own territory, Carolina needed another big play. On third down, the Panthers got it. Delhomme found Muhsin Muhammad for an 85-yard touchdown pass. It set a Super Bowl record for the longest play from scrimmage. The Panthers took a 22–21 lead. Again, Carolina went for a two-point conversion but failed.

The lead did not last long. Brady drove the Patriots down the field. He threw a 1-yard touchdown pass to Mike Vrabel. They then scored on a two-point conversion. Carolina was down by seven points with 2:51 left.

But the Panthers had been called the "Cardiac Cats" because they had rallied for so many heart-stopping wins

MUHSIN MUHAMMAD SCORES ON AN 85-YARD TOUCHDOWN RECEPTION IN THE FOURTH QUARTER TO GIVE THE PANTHERS A LEAD IN THE SUPER BOWL.

during the regular season. They had come this far. Carolina was not going to fold now.

Delhomme marched the Panthers down the field. His 12-yard touchdown pass to Ricky Proehl, followed by Kasay's extra point, tied the score at 29–29. There was only 1:08 left to play.

Unfortunately for Carolina, New England had enough time to try to advance the ball into field-goal range. Brady had led the Patriots on a game-winning drive two years earlier in the Super Bowl against the St. Louis Rams. Against the Panthers, he also was able to make key plays down the stretch. The final one was a 17-yard pass to Deion Branch on third-and-three to give New England a shot at a field goal. Adam Vinatieri had made a Super Bowl-winning kick two years earlier. He came through in the clutch again with a 41-yard field goal. There were only four seconds remaining. The Panthers could not return the following kickoff for a touchdown. The Patriots won 32–29 in a classic Super Bowl. The "Cardiac Cats" were heartbroken.

POSTSEASON PATH

Carolina's playoff road to the Super Bowl after the 2003 season was not easy. The Panthers beat the visiting Dallas Cowboys 29–10 in the wild-card round. But then things got much trickier. Next up was a road game against the St. Louis Rams. Jake Delhomme's 69-yard touchdown pass to Steve Smith gave the Panthers a thrilling 29–23 win in double overtime. The Panthers then faced the host Philadelphia Eagles in the NFC Championship Game. The Eagles had defeated the Panthers 25–16 in Charlotte, North Carolina, late in the regular season. Carolina would not be denied this time, though. Stephen Davis and DeShaun Foster combined for 136 rushing yards and a touchdown. Panthers rookie cornerback Ricky Manning Jr. intercepted three passes by Eagles quarterback Donovan McNabb. Carolina recorded five sacks. The Panthers won 14–3 to clinch their first Super Bowl appearance.

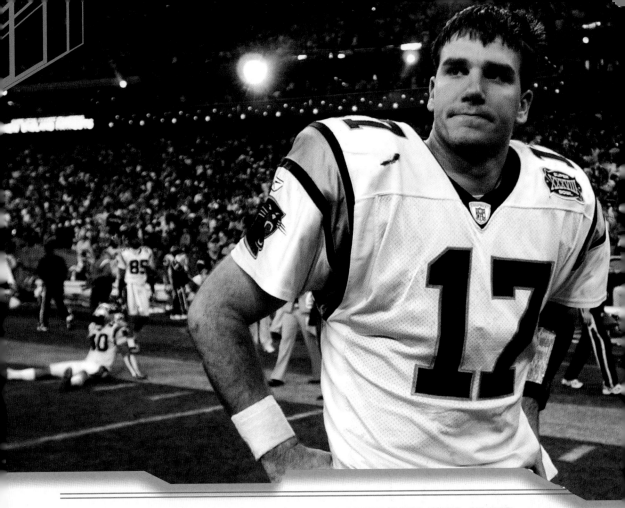

JAKE DELHOMME REACTS AFTER CAROLINA'S SUPER BOWL LOSS. AT THE TIME, HIS 323 PASSING YARDS WERE HIS SECOND MOST IN AN NFL GAME.

Panthers coach John Fox had praise for his quarterback. Delhomme finished 16-for-33 for 323 yards and three touchdowns with no interceptions. "I thought he kept us in the game," Fox said. "Unfortunately, [the Patriots] had the ball last."

Carolina's remarkable season had not ended the way the team wanted. But the Panthers had come a long way for a team that had struggled so much just two years earlier and had only begun playing in the NFL in 1995.

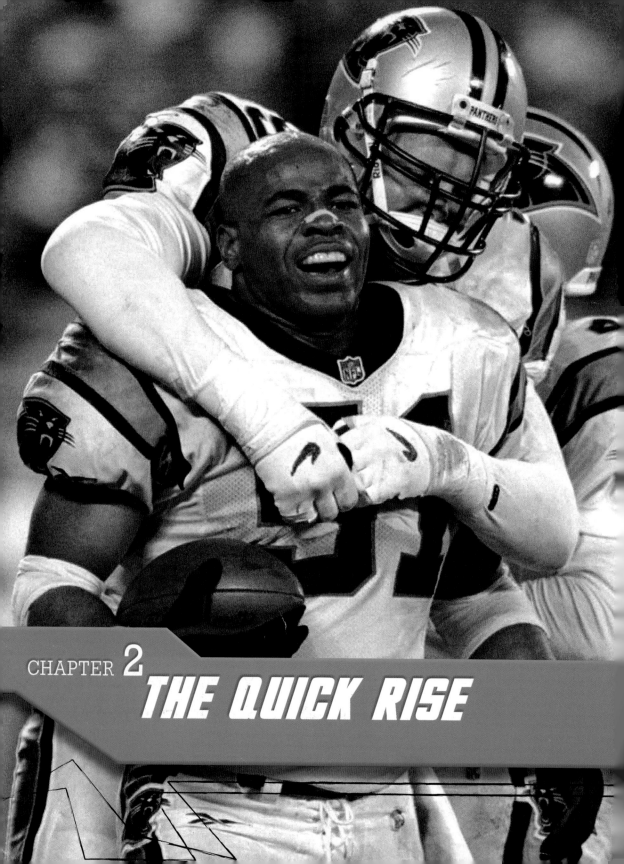

CHAPTER 2
THE QUICK RISE

In 1987, the NFL announced plans to allow two expansion teams into the league. Eleven cities or regions applied to join the NFL. North Carolina native Jerry Richardson headed a group representing the Carolinas—North Carolina and South Carolina. The group was called Richardson Sports.

Richardson had played as a wide receiver for the NFL's Baltimore Colts in 1959 and 1960. He caught a 12-yard touchdown pass from Johnny Unitas in the 1959 NFL Championship Game. It helped the Colts beat the New York Giants 31–16. After his NFL playing career, Richardson became a successful businessman.

FAST-FOOD KING

Jerry Richardson took the $3,500 he earned from competing in NFL playoff games with the Baltimore Colts and cofounded Spartan Foods in 1961. The company began to operate Hardee's fast-food restaurants. The group had the second Hardee's franchise and was so successful that it ended up running 385 Hardee's stores. Richardson built his fortune this way.

LINEBACKER SAM MILLS IS HUGGED BY OFFENSIVE LINEMAN MATT ELLIOTT DURING CAROLINA'S 26–17 PLAYOFF WIN OVER DALLAS IN JANUARY 1997.

Richardson's goal was to bring an NFL team to the Carolinas. He convinced the league to hold three exhibition games in the region, in 1989, 1990, and 1991. Each game sold out. The NFL cut down the list of possible expansion cities to five. The Carolina group advanced.

Richardson's group decided that the potential team would play in Charlotte, North Carolina. Then the group determined that it needed a new stadium to help strengthen its case with the NFL. Richardson Sports would sell public seat licenses (PSLs) to pay for a new stadium. Fans who wanted to buy tickets would have to purchase PSLs.

The NFL liked the idea but wanted to make sure that the people in the Carolinas would pay for the PSLs. In two months, more than $112 million was raised. The plan worked.

On October 26, 1993, the NFL announced that it was awarding the league's twenty-ninth franchise to the Carolinas. The team would begin play in 1995. Jacksonville, Florida, received the other expansion team the next month.

After years of work, the Carolinas had an NFL team. The nickname Panthers and the team colors of black, blue, and silver were chosen. The team would go by the name Carolina Panthers.

Next, Dom Capers was selected to be Carolina's first coach. Capers had been a successful defensive coordinator for the Pittsburgh Steelers.

Then the Panthers stocked their roster from three main sources. First, the existing NFL teams made players available to Carolina and Jacksonville in an

PANTHERS OWNER JERRY RICHARDSON, SHOWN IN 2000, SAW HIS DREAM
OF AN NFL TEAM IN THE CAROLINAS COME TRUE.

expansion draft. The Panthers added 35 players through this process. They included cornerback Tim McKyer, who would become an early team leader.

Next up was the draft of college players—the NFL Draft. Carolina added 11 players to its roster this way. Among them was former Penn State University star quarterback Kerry Collins. Collins was the Panthers' first draft choice. He was taken fifth overall after the team traded the second selection to the Cincinnati Bengals for the fifth pick and a second-round choice.

Carolina also signed free agents. The Panthers picked up some of the top players for

their debut season through this method, including linebackers Darion Conner, Lamar Lathon, and Sam Mills.

The Panthers were placed in the NFC West Division. The other teams in the division were the Atlanta Falcons, New Orleans Saints, San Francisco 49ers, and St. Louis Rams.

The Panthers struggled initially, losing their first five games. Then Carolina defeated the visiting New York Jets 26–15 on October 15 for its first regular-season win. John Kasay kicked four field goals. The Panthers played their home games in 1995 at Memorial Stadium on the Clemson University campus in Clemson,

COACH DOM CAPERS AND LINEBACKER LAMAR LATHON ARE ALL SMILES AFTER THE PANTHERS BEAT THE JETS IN OCTOBER 1995 FOR THEIR FIRST REGULAR-SEASON VICTORY EVER.

SAM MILLS

The Cleveland Browns signed linebacker Sam Mills, a former star at Montclair State in New Jersey, as an undrafted free agent in 1981. But the Browns released him. They thought the 5-foot-9 Mills was too short.

Mills went on to play three seasons in the United States Football League. It was a rival league to the NFL. He then signed with the New Orleans Saints and would play 12 NFL seasons. He made five Pro Bowls. Mills signed with the expansion Panthers in 1995. He played with them through 1997 before retiring.

After he retired, Mills stayed with the Panthers as linebackers coach. He was diagnosed with intestinal cancer during the 2003 season but continued to coach. Mills was an inspiration for Carolina during its Super Bowl run that season. Mills passed away on April 18, 2005, at 45.

A statue of Mills greets visitors at Carolina's Bank of America Stadium.

South Carolina. The team's new stadium was still being built in Charlotte and would not open until 1996.

The victory over the Jets was the start of a four-game winning streak. The Panthers finished their first season 7–9. It was the most wins ever by an expansion team. Carolina became known around the NFL as a very good defensive team.

Things went even better for the Panthers in their second season. Before it started, they signed veteran linebacker Kevin Greene. Greene had been a star with the Los Angeles Rams and the Pittsburgh Steelers.

The Panthers were now playing at the brand-new Ericsson Stadium (it would later be renamed Bank of America Stadium) in Charlotte. Carolina routed Atlanta 29–6 in the first regular-season game at the new stadium on September 1, 1996. The Panthers finished very strongly with a seven-game winning streak. This gave Carolina a surprising 12–4 record and the NFC West title.

Collins finished with 14 touchdown passes against nine interceptions. Tight end Wesley Walls had 61 receptions, 10 of them for touchdowns. Greene finished with 14.5 sacks. Lathon had 13.5. Anthony Johnson rushed for 1,120 yards. Michael Bates's average of 30.2 yards per kickoff return led the NFL.

In the playoffs, Carolina received a bye in the first round. The Panthers then hosted the Dallas Cowboys. The Cowboys had won three of the previous four Super Bowls. They were getting older, however. Collins threw for two touchdowns and

ADDING LINEBACKER KEVIN GREENE IN 1996 HELPED THE PANTHERS
BECOME ONE OF THE NFL'S TOP TEAMS IN JUST THEIR SECOND SEASON.

Kasay made four field goals as Carolina won 26–17.

The Panthers went to chilly Green Bay to face the Packers and star quarterback Brett Favre in the NFC Championship Game. Carolina jumped out to an early lead behind a touchdown pass by Collins. But the Panthers' defense had no answer for the Packers' powerful offense.

Green Bay rolled to a 30–13 victory. The Packers went on to win the Super Bowl.

Carolina appeared to be a team on the rise. The defense had continued to play very well. It gave up the second-fewest points in the NFL.

But the Panthers would discover that continued success in the NFL does not come easily.

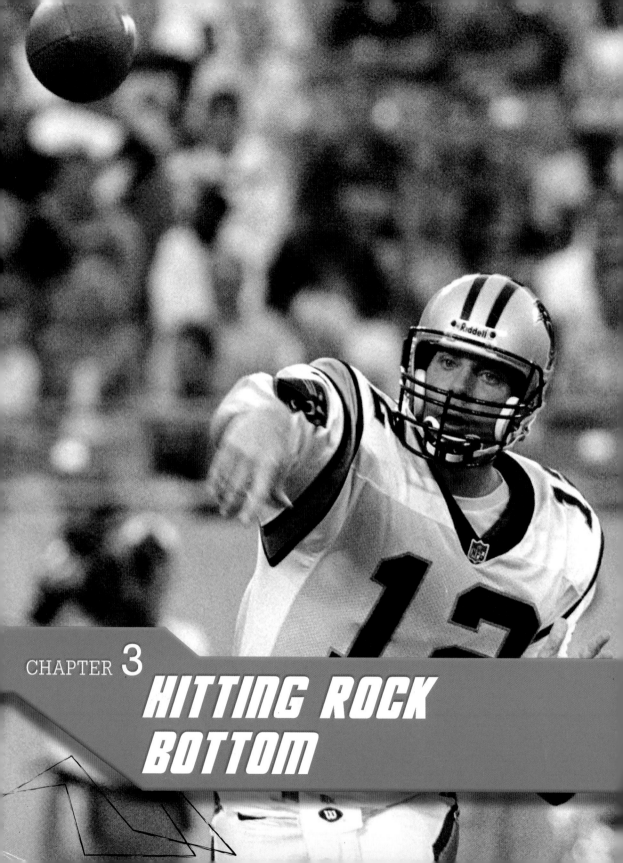

CHAPTER 3

HITTING ROCK BOTTOM

The good feelings from the 1996 season did not last long for the Panthers. Star linebacker Kevin Greene held out for more money. Carolina released him. He ended up with the San Francisco 49ers. Linebacker Sam Mills, at age 38, finally started to slow down. He retired at the end of the 1997 season. Linebacker Lamar Lathon did not have a strong year.

As a result of all those things, the Panthers struggled in 1997. Carolina finished 7–9 and missed the playoffs.

Greene returned to the Panthers for the 1998 season. He was just as dominant as he had been in 1996. But Carolina fell apart.

THEY SAID IT

"*I never intended to quit the team. I intended to discuss the situation with [coach Dom Capers]. I was at a time in my life where I was confused about a lot of things.*"
—Former Panthers quarterback Kerry Collins, on the 1998 season

KERRY COLLINS PASSES DURING AN EXHIBITION GAME IN 1998. COLLINS PLAYED IN JUST FOUR REGULAR-SEASON GAMES FOR THE PANTHERS THAT YEAR BEFORE THE TEAM RELEASED HIM.

QUARTERBACK STEVE BEUERLEIN AND COACH GEORGE SEIFERT CONSULT ON THE SIDELINE DURING A GAME IN 1999.

The Panthers started poorly. Quarterback Kerry Collins asked to be taken out of the lineup. Coach Dom Capers, thinking Collins quit the team, had Carolina release Collins. Collins joined New Orleans for the rest of 1998. He would go on to play for the New York Giants the next season. Collins later acknowledged that his erratic behavior with the Panthers was the result of struggling with alcoholism. He underwent treatment.

Capers made Steve Beuerlein the starting quarterback for the rest of 1998. The Panthers fell all the way to 0–7 before they finally earned their first win of the year. Carolina won its final two games to finish 4–12.

One day after the 1998 season, Carolina fired Capers. The team hired former San Francisco coach George Seifert. Seifert went 98–30 with the 49ers from 1989 to 1996. Like Capers, Seifert was known as a defense-oriented coach.

Carolina struggled at the beginning of the 1999 season. But the Panthers ended the year on a high note by winning three of their final four games. They finished 8–8. The big surprise was that Carolina won with offense. The Panthers averaged nearly 35 points in those final four games. Beuerlein set a team record with 36 touchdown passes and made the Pro Bowl. Wide receiver Muhsin Muhammad and tight end Wesley Walls also made the Pro Bowl.

But the Panthers struggled in 2000 and went 7–9. For the first time in Seifert's coaching career, one of his teams finished below .500. In the final game of the season, Carolina suffered its biggest defeat ever. The Panthers lost 52–9 to the host Oakland Raiders on Christmas Eve.

MUHSIN MUHAMMAD

The Panthers selected former Michigan State University wide receiver Muhsin Muhammad in the second round of the 1996 NFL Draft. He became a full-time starter with Carolina in 1998. He developed into one of the NFL's top receivers. In 1999 and 2000, Muhammad had back-to-back seasons with more than 1,000 receiving yards. He set a team record with 96 receptions in 1999 and broke it the next year with 102. After leading the NFL with 1,405 receiving yards and 16 touchdown catches in 2004, he joined Chicago as a free agent. Muhammad played three seasons with the Bears. But he did not have the success that he enjoyed with the Panthers. He rejoined Carolina before the 2008 season.

The worst was still to come. The Panthers won their season opener in 2001. But they went on to lose their next 15 games and finished with a miserable 1–15 record. Carolina lost in every way imaginable. Chris Weinke, a 29-year-old rookie who had won the Heisman Trophy at Florida State University, was the Panthers' starting quarterback that year.

After the season, Carolina fired Seifert. John Fox became the third coach in team history. Again, the Panthers hired a defensive-minded coach. Fox had been the New York Giants' defensive coordinator. He helped New York reach Super Bowl XXXV after the 2000 season.

QUARTERBACK CHRIS WEINKE TRIES TO GET RID OF THE BALL IN 2001. THE PANTHERS FINISHED 1–15 THAT SEASON.

RAE CARRUTH

Rae Carruth seemed to have the world at his feet. Then everything went horribly wrong.

Carruth, a former University of Colorado star, had four touchdown catches as a rookie wide receiver with the Panthers in 1997. Injuries limited him the next two seasons. But it was an off-the-field incident that ended his career.

On November 16, 1999, a car pulled next to the car of Cherica Adams, Carruth's girlfriend. Adams, who was eight months pregnant with Carruth's child, was shot four times. She dialed 9-1-1 and said she believed Carruth was involved. Adams's baby was saved, but Adams died.

The police arrested Carruth. A trial began on October 23, 2000, and lasted 27 days. Carruth was convicted of conspiracy to commit murder, shooting into an occupied vehicle, and using an instrument to destroy an unborn child. He was sentenced to 18 to 24 years in prison.

THE RETURN
TO GLORY

The Panthers did not have much success in George Seifert's three seasons coaching the team, from 1999 to 2001. However, during that time they did add some important players who would help the squad flourish in 2003.

In all, 12 starters on the 2003 Panthers Super Bowl team came aboard during Seifert's time with the team. They included defensive tackle Kris Jenkins, linebacker Dan Morgan, and wide receiver Steve Smith—all of whom were selected in the 2001 NFL Draft.

In 2002, the Panthers found themselves with a new coach,

JOHN FOX

When the Panthers hired John Fox as coach in January 2002, he was given a difficult task: turn around a team that went 1–15 in 2001. Fox's background was as a defensive coach. He had been a defensive coordinator with the Los Angeles/Oakland Raiders (1994–95) and the New York Giants (1997–2001). With the Panthers, Fox made defense his first focus. Under Fox's guidance, Carolina's defense improved greatly right away in 2002. Defense would remain a team strength the rest of the decade under Fox.

RUNNING BACK STEPHEN DAVIS AND COACH JOHN FOX EMBRACE AFTER THE 2003 PANTHERS' NFC TITLE GAME WIN IN PHILADELPHIA.

JULIUS PEPPERS

One of the reasons Carolina improved on defense in 2002 was the addition of Julius Peppers. The Panthers selected the defensive end in the first round, second overall, in the 2002 NFL Draft.

Peppers was a North Carolina native and had starred at the University of North Carolina in Chapel Hill. He was a remarkable athlete. In addition to excelling on the gridiron, the 6-foot-6, 280-pound Peppers played for the Tar Heels' renowned basketball program.

Peppers was very strong and fast. He had 12 sacks in 2002 and was named the NFL's Defensive Rookie of the Year.

Peppers would continue to torment NFL offenses. He had 10 sacks or more in six of his eight seasons with Carolina. Peppers was selected to five Pro Bowls with the Panthers.

In March 2010, he signed a six-year contract worth $91.5 million with the Chicago Bears.

John Fox, and in a new division. Since joining the NFL, Carolina had played in the NFC West. But with the addition of the expansion Houston Texans in 2002, the NFL went from six divisions to eight. The new NFC South had three former NFC West teams in Carolina, Atlanta, and New Orleans. The Tampa Bay Buccaneers were the final NFC South team. They had previously played in the NFC Central.

Carolina won its first three games under Fox in 2002. But then it felt like 2001 all over again. The Panthers lost eight games in a row. However, Carolina rebounded to win four of its final five games. The Panthers finished 7–9. NFL veteran Rodney Peete was Carolina's starting quarterback in 2002. He threw for 15 touchdowns with 14 interceptions.

COACH JOHN FOX AND JULIUS PEPPERS HOLD UP PEPPERS'S NEW JERSEY IN APRIL 2002 AFTER THE PANTHERS DRAFTED THE DEFENSIVE END.

The Panthers' defensive improvement under Fox was immediate. They gave up the fifth-fewest points in the NFL in 2002. In 2001, they ranked twenty-eighth in that category. However, Carolina's offense continued to struggle in 2002.

In an attempt to improve the offense, Fox brought in two key free agents before the 2003 season: running back Stephen Davis and quarterback Jake Delhomme. Davis was coming off four strong seasons in a row with the Washington Redskins.

Delhomme was stuck on the bench with New Orleans. But Fox had liked what he had seen of Delhomme.

Both signings worked out very well. Davis set a Carolina record for rushing yards in a season with 1,444. Delhomme, meanwhile, took over for Peete during the first game of the season and remained the starter.

Behind their new stars, the Panthers climbed from thirtieth in the NFL in points scored to fifteenth. Combined with its strong defense, Carolina finished the year 11–5 and in first place in the NFC South. The team peaked at the right time and made its magical run to the Super Bowl.

Injuries kept the Panthers from repeating that kind of success the next season. Smith broke his leg in the first game. Davis suffered a knee injury shortly thereafter. Carolina got off to a 1–7 start. However, the Panthers rebounded to win six of their final eight games to go 7–9. Delhomme continued to play well.

The Panthers were healthy again in 2005. They rebounded

STEPHEN DAVIS

The Washington Redskins selected 6-foot, 230-pound running back Stephen Davis in the fourth round of the 1996 NFL Draft. The former Auburn University star had a breakout season in 1999 with 1,405 rushing yards. He reached 1,300 yards in three of the next four seasons as well. Davis dislocated a shoulder in 2002 and missed four games. The Redskins let him go as a free agent. The South Carolina native signed with the Panthers and rushed for a career-high 1,444 yards in 2003. In the playoffs, Davis added 315 yards and a touchdown rushing despite battling injuries. Knee injuries limited Davis to 204 carries over the next two seasons. He left to play for the St. Louis Rams in 2006 but retired after that season. Davis had just one big year for the Panthers. But he was a key reason the 2003 team made it all the way to the Super Bowl.

STEVE SMITH CELEBRATES HIS 69-YARD TOUCHDOWN RECEPTION THAT GAVE CAROLINA A 29–23 PLAYOFF WIN AT ST. LOUIS IN JANUARY 2004.

to win the NFC South with an 11–5 record. Smith had the best year of his career and won the NFL Comeback Player of the Year award.

Carolina reached its third NFC Championship Game in team history thanks to road victories over the New York Giants (23–0) and the Chicago Bears

(29–21). Third-year running back DeShaun Foster rushed for 151 yards for the Panthers against the Giants. In the Bears game, Smith had 12 catches for 218 yards and two touchdowns.

Carolina, though, ran out of steam in the NFC title contest. Quarterback Matt Hasselbeck and running back Shaun Alexander led the Seattle Seahawks to a 34–14 victory over the visiting Panthers. The Seahawks intercepted three of Delhomme's passes. Seattle finished a 10–0 season at home—going 8–0 in the regular season and 2–0 in the playoffs. The Seahawks would lose 21–10 to the Pittsburgh Steelers in the Super Bowl.

The Panthers were disappointed in the way the season had ended. Still, they had advanced as far as the NFC title game for the second time in three seasons and had won two NFC South crowns during that time. They figured that more bright days were ahead.

STEVE SMITH

The Panthers originally used Steve Smith as primarily a kick returner. The former University of Utah standout scored three touchdowns on returns in his rookie season in 2001. By 2003, the speedy Smith had developed into an excellent starting wide receiver. He had 88 catches for 1,110 yards and seven touchdowns. He helped the Panthers reach the Super Bowl. Smith broke his leg in the 2004 opener and missed the rest of the season. He rebounded in 2005. The 5-foot-9, 185-pound Smith set team records with 103 catches and 1,563 receiving yards. He had 12 touchdown receptions. The receiving yards were the most in the NFL. The reception and touchdown catch totals were tied for league highs. As a result, Smith accomplished the rare "Triple Crown" receiving feat. He was the first player to achieve it since Green Bay's Sterling Sharpe in 1992.

RUNNING BACK DESHAUN FOSTER BREAKS AWAY FROM A GIANTS DEFENDER IN THE PANTHERS' WILD-CARD PLAYOFF VICTORY IN JANUARY 2006.

CHAPTER 5

DOUBLE TROUBLE

Going into the 2006 season, the Panthers had high hopes. They had won two NFC South Division titles in the previous three seasons. They had reached the Super Bowl after the 2003 season and narrowly lost. In the playoffs after the 2005 season, they finished one game short of making it back to the Super Bowl.

Injuries to wide receiver Steve Smith and quarterback Jake Delhomme, however, made the 2006 campaign frustrating. The Panthers finished 8–8. It was more of the same in 2007. Delhomme was injured in the third game and missed the rest of the year. The right-hander had ligament replacement surgery in his throwing arm. Carolina went 7–9.

The Panthers looked forward to Delhomme's return in 2008. An incident during training camp threatened to distract the team, however. On August 1, Smith and teammate Ken Lucas, a cornerback, got into a fight.

PANTHERS RUNNING BACKS JONATHAN STEWART AND DEANGELO WILLIAMS, KNOWN AS "DOUBLE TROUBLE," CELEBRATE IN DECEMBER 2008.

Smith broke Lucas's nose. Smith reportedly apologized to Lucas the day of the scuffle. But the team sent Smith home and eventually decided to suspend him for the first two regular-season games.

Despite missing the first two games, Smith had a fine season. He finished with 78 catches for 1,421 yards and six touchdowns. He was selected to the Pro Bowl.

But the biggest story of the 2008 season for the Panthers was the emergence of two young running backs who helped the team get back to the playoffs. Many wondered whether DeAngelo Williams or Jonathan Stewart would be the team's main runner. Coach John Fox ended up featuring both backs. The youngsters became known as "Double Trouble."

Carolina selected Williams in the first round, twenty-seventh overall, in the 2006 NFL Draft. The former University of Memphis star was a backup to DeShaun Foster during his first two years in the NFL. The Panthers chose Stewart in the first round, thirteenth overall, in the 2008 draft. Stewart had been a University of Oregon standout.

THEY SAID IT

"*Sometimes it takes a little adversity. If it wasn't for the adversity, I don't know if me and Steve would have the relationship we do now. Now I can truly say we're friends. I don't regret any moment of it. I had to be a sacrificial offering, but at the same time it was for a bigger cause, like I told the world it would be.*"
—Former Panthers cornerback Ken Lucas, reflecting on his 2008 training camp fight with Steve Smith

CAROLINA'S DEANGELO WILLIAMS BREAKS AWAY FOR A BIG GAIN. WILLIAMS'S 1,515 RUSHING YARDS IN 2008 WERE MORE THAN DOUBLE WHAT HE HAD THE PREVIOUS SEASON.

Fox decided to split carries between the two backs. Williams was officially the starter. But Stewart would receive more playing time than a typical backup.

Williams ran for three touchdowns as Carolina defeated the visiting Kansas City Chiefs 34–0 to improve to 4–1. It was the first of five games in 2008 in which Williams would score at least two touchdowns. He finished the season with 1,515 rushing yards, breaking Stephen Davis's team record. He also scored 20 touchdowns (18 rushing, two receiving) to top Muhsin Muhammad's Panthers mark of 16, set in 2004.

Stewart, meanwhile, finished his rookie season with 836 yards and 10 touchdowns rushing. He and Williams led the Panthers to a 12–4 record and an NFC South title.

Carolina hosted the Arizona Cardinals in the playoffs' divisional round. Stewart opened the scoring with a 9-yard touchdown run. But then the Cardinals scored the next 33 points. Arizona's stars, quarterback Kurt Warner and wide receiver Larry Fitzgerald, had big games. The Cardinals advanced with a 33–13 victory. The Panthers were disappointed that they had not played better, especially considering that the game was at home. Delhomme had a very poor performance. He threw five interceptions. Carolina committed six turnovers in all. The Cardinals would eventually advance to the Super Bowl. Arizona was edged 27–23 by Pittsburgh.

THE CARDINALS' CALAIS CAMPBELL CONTESTS QUARTERBACK JAKE DELHOMME'S PASS DURING A PLAYOFF GAME IN JANUARY 2009. THE PANTHERS LOST 33–13.

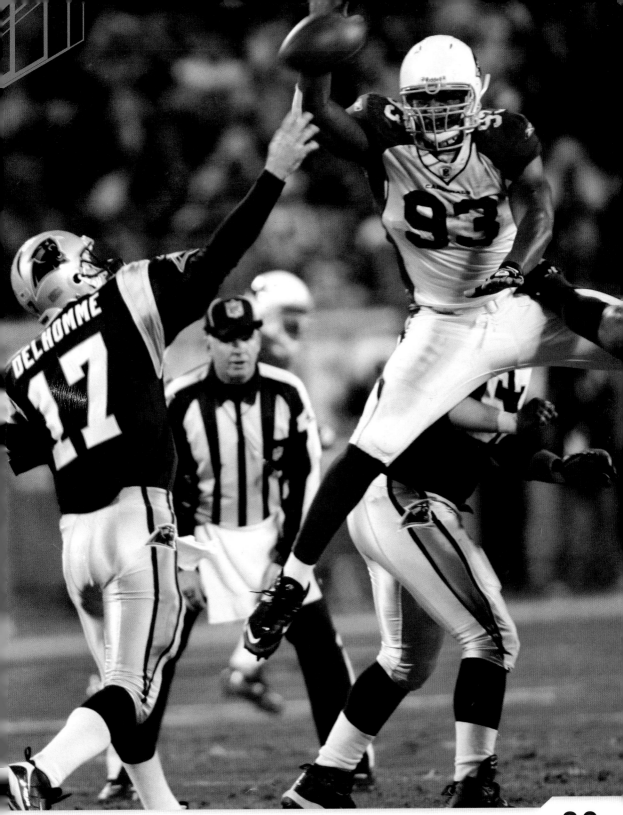

Double Trouble had another big season for the Panthers in 2009. Stewart set a team record with 206 rushing yards in a 41–9 win over the New York Giants. He finished the season with 1,133 rushing yards and 11 total touchdowns. Williams, meanwhile, ran for 1,117 yards and seven touchdowns despite battling injuries and missing three games. Stewart and Williams became just the sixth duo in NFL history in which both players ran for 1,000 yards in the same season. They were the first to both top 1,100 yards. The Panthers finished 8–8 and missed the playoffs. But the play of the Double Trouble tandem continued to give Panthers fans hope for the future.

Delhomme's performance in 2009, however, was disappointing. Before the season, Carolina signed Delhomme to a five-year contract extension worth $42.5 million. Delhomme finished the season with just eight touchdown passes against 18 interceptions in 11 games. Matt Moore was the team's starting quarterback by the end of the year. He played well, and the Panthers won their final three games.

On March 5, 2010, the Panthers made the difficult decision to release Delhomme. The team felt that it was time to go in another direction. Delhomme signed with the Cleveland Browns shortly thereafter.

March 5 was a big news day for the Panthers for another reason. Julius Peppers, the team's dynamic defensive end, signed a six-year, $91.5 million contract with the Chicago Bears.

Carolina would proceed into the future without its two most recognizable players of

QUARTERBACK JAKE DELHOMME IS OVERCOME WITH EMOTION DURING A NEWS CONFERENCE IN MARCH 2010 IN WHICH HE DISCUSSED BEING RELEASED BY THE PANTHERS.

recent years. But the team still had Double Trouble, and that spelled trouble for the rest of the NFL. The Panthers hoped that Stewart and Williams could lead the team back to another Super Bowl, with the ultimate goal of winning it for the first time.

TIMELINE

1993	On October 26, the NFL awards Jerry Richardson's ownership group the first of two expansion franchises that will begin play in the 1995 season. The team will be called the Carolina Panthers.
1995	The Panthers hire former Pittsburgh Steelers defensive coordinator Dom Capers as their first coach on January 23.
1995	The Panthers play their first regular-season game and lose 23–20 in overtime to the host Atlanta Falcons on September 3.
1995	On October 15, Carolina beats the New York Jets 26–15 at Clemson University in Clemson, South Carolina, to win its first regular-season game.
1996	The Panthers open their brand-new stadium, then called Ericsson Stadium, for an exhibition game against the Chicago Bears and win 30–12 on August 3.
1997	On January 5, host Carolina earns its first playoff win on its first try with a 26–17 victory over the Dallas Cowboys.
1999	Former San Francisco 49ers coach George Seifert is hired to replace Capers as the Panthers' second coach on January 4. Carolina let go of Capers at the end of the 1998 season.
2002	Former New York Giants defensive coordinator John Fox becomes the Panthers' third coach on January 25. The team fired Seifert after the 2001 season, in which Carolina went 1–15.

2002	With the second overall pick in the NFL Draft, the Panthers select Julius Peppers from the University of North Carolina on April 20. Peppers goes on to make five Pro Bowls in his eight years with the team.
2004	The Panthers capture their first NFC title with a 14–3 road win over the Philadelphia Eagles on January 18.
2004	In its first Super Bowl, Carolina is edged 32–29 by the New England Patriots when Adam Vinatieri kicks a 41-yard field goal with four seconds left at Reliant Stadium in Houston, Texas, on February 1. The Panthers' Jake Delhomme throws for 323 yards and three touchdowns.
2005	Former Panthers linebacker Sam Mills passes away on April 18 at the age of 45 after a fight with intestinal cancer. Mills also served as an assistant coach with Carolina after his playing career. On August 13, the team honors Mills and his number 51 by retiring it.
2006	The Panthers tie an NFL record with their fourth straight road victory in the playoffs with a 29–21 win over the Chicago Bears on January 15.
2008	On December 14, Carolina beats the Denver Broncos 30–10 to finish the regular season 8–0 at home for the second time in team history. The Panthers also accomplished that feat in 1996.
2010	Jonathan Stewart rushes for 125 yards in the Panthers' 23–10 win over the visiting New Orleans Saints in the regular-season finale on January 3. The performance puts Stewart's season rushing total at 1,133 yards. He and DeAngelo Williams become the first teammates to rush for 1,100 yards in the same season.

QUICK STATS

FRANCHISE HISTORY
1995–

SUPER BOWLS
2003 (XXXVIII)

DIVISION CHAMPIONSHIPS
1996, 2003, 2005, 2008

PLAYOFF APPEARANCES
1996, 2003, 2005, 2008

KEY PLAYERS
(position, seasons with team)

Michael Bates (KR/DB, 1996–2000)
Kerry Collins (QB, 1995–98)
Jake Delhomme (QB, 2003–09)
Kevin Greene (LB, 1996, 1998–99)
John Kasay (K, 1995–)
Sam Mills (LB, 1995–97)
Mike Minter (S, 1997–2006)
Muhsin Muhammad
    (WR, 1996–2004, 2008–)
Julius Peppers (DE, 2002–09)
Mike Rucker (DE, 1999–2007)
Steve Smith (WR, 2001–)
Wesley Walls (TE, 1996–2002)

KEY COACHES

Dom Capers (1995–98):
    30–34–0; 1–1 (playoffs)
John Fox (2002–):
    71–57–0; 5–3 (playoffs)

HOME FIELDS

Bank of America Stadium (1996–)
    Known as Ericsson Stadium
    1996–2003
Clemson Memorial Stadium (1995)

* All statistics through 2009 season

QUOTES AND ANECDOTES

"Kicking a football is very simple. I did it in my backyard at the age of 4. But put 11 guys on the other side, fill the stadium with 70,000 screaming fans, battle it out for three hours, and have the outcome of the game determined by that final kick—it's no longer quite so simple."
—Carolina place-kicker John Kasay

John Kasay was a fourth-round pick of the Seattle Seahawks in 1991. The left-footed kicker played at the University of Georgia. He spent four seasons with Seattle before joining Carolina in time for its first season in 1995. Through 2009, he was still with the Panthers. Kasay immediately established his worth with Carolina by making three game-winning kicks in 1995. In 1996, Kasay led the NFL with 145 points and made 37 field goals to set a record, which has since been broken. On December 6, 2009, Kasay made the 400th field goal of his career. He became only the seventh player in NFL history to accomplish the feat.

"Sam was one of the finest people you will ever meet. You would never know that he was a player who made Pro Bowls and had all this attention because he treated everybody the same no matter who they were. He never had a bad thing to say about anybody and had a great ability to laugh at himself. He was the type of guy you want your kids to grow up to be."
—Carolina general manager Marty Hurney, on former Panthers linebacker Sam Mills. Mills passed away on April 18, 2005, after a battle with cancer.

Which Panthers player is the great-nephew of a Motown singing legend? The answer is guard Duke Robinson. Smokey Robinson is his great-uncle.

GLOSSARY

bye

The position of a team or person in a tournament that advances to the next round without playing.

contract

A binding agreement about, for example, years of commitment by a football player in exchange for a given salary.

draft

A system used by professional sports leagues to select new players in order to spread incoming talent among all teams.

dynamic

Marked by intensity and vigor, capable of making big things happen.

exhibition game

A game, typically played before the official start of the season, that does not factor into the standings.

expansion

In sports, to add a franchise or franchises to a league.

franchise

An entire sports organization, including the players, coaches, and staff.

general manager

The executive who is in charge of the team's overall operation. He or she hires and fires coaches, drafts college players, and signs free agents.

Heisman Trophy

An award given to the top college football player each year.

ligament

A band of tissue that connects bones or holds organs in place.

Pro Bowl

A game after the regular season in which the top players from the AFC play against the top players from the NFC.

torment

To make things very difficult for another person or team.

FOR MORE INFORMATION

Further Reading

Charlotte Observer. *Cardiac Cats: Carolina's Unforgettable 2003 Season.* Chicago: Triumph Books, 2004.

MacCambridge, Michael. *America's Game: The Epic Story of How Pro Football Captured a Nation.* New York: Random House, 2004.

Rosinski, Bill, and Pat Yasinskas. *Bill Rosinski's Tales from the Carolina Panthers.* Champaign, IL: Sports Publishing LLC, 2007.

Web Links

To learn more about the Carolina Panthers, visit ABDO Publishing Company online at **www.abdopublishing.com.** Web sites about the Panthers are featured on our Book Links page. These links are routinely monitored and updated to provide the most current information available.

Places to Visit

Bank of America Stadium
800 South Mint Street
Charlotte, NC 28202
704-358-7407
The home of the Carolina Panthers is a 73,778-seat open-air stadium. Look for statues honoring former general manager and president Mike McCormack and linebacker Sam Mills.

Pro Football Hall of Fame
2121 George Halas Drive Northwest
Canton, OH 44708
330-456-8207
This hall of fame and museum highlights the greatest players and moments in the history of the National Football League. As of 2010, no one affiliated with the Panthers had been enshrined.

Wofford College
Richardson Athletic Building
429 North Church Street
Spartanburg, SC 29303
864-597-4090
Wofford College is home of the Panthers' summer training camp. Richardson Athletic Building is where the players stay during camp.

INDEX

About the Author

Brian Joura is a freelance writer. In addition to the Carolina Panthers, he has covered the Charlotte Bobcats, the Atlantic Coast Conference and NCAA basketball tournaments, the Meineke Car Care Bowl, the Greensboro Grasshoppers, and the Carolina Dynamo. Joura is also the official scorer for the Asheboro Copperheads. He is a featured writer at RotoGraphs and also writes for FantasyPros911.com and Mets360.com. Joura lives with his family in North Carolina.